The American Journey

D1091481

Chapter Summaries

GLENCOE

McGraw-Hill

New York, New York   Columbus, Ohio   Woodland Hills, California   Peoria, Illinois

To the Teacher

The American Journey Chapter Summaries booklet provides a condensed version of the important information in each chapter of *The American Journey*. These summaries can be used as a quick review of chapter content or as make-up work. Each summary ends with a Think-About-It question.

Customize Your Resources

No matter how you organize your teaching resources, Glencoe has what you need.

The **Teacher's Classroom Resources** for *The American Journey* provides you with a wide variety of supplemental materials to enhance the classroom experience. These resources appear as individual booklets in a carryall tote box. The booklets are designed to open flat so that pages can be easily photocopied without removing them from their booklet. However, if you choose to create separate files, the pages are perforated for easy removal. You may customize these materials using our file folders or tabbed dividers.

The individual booklets and the file management kit supplied in **Teacher's Classroom Resources** give you the flexibility to organize these resources in a combination that best suits your teaching style. Below are several alternatives:

- **Organize all resources by category**
  (all tests, all history themes activities, all cooperative learning activities, etc., filed separately)

- **Organize all resources by category and chapter**
  (all Chapter 1 activities, all Chapter 1 tests, etc.)

- **Organize resources sequentially by lesson**
  (activities, quizzes, readings, etc., for Chapter 1, Chapter 2, and so on)

Glencoe/McGraw-Hill

A Division of The McGraw·Hill Companies

Send all inquiries to:
Glencoe/McGraw-Hill
8787 Orion Place
Columbus, OH 43240

ISBN 0-07-820811-4

Printed in the United States of America

2 3 4 5 6 7 8 9 10 066 03 02 01 00

Table of Contents

To the Teacher ii

Chapter Summaries

Chapter Summary 1   The First Americans 1

Chapter Summary 2   Exploring the Americas 2

Chapter Summary 3   Colonial America 3

Chapter Summary 4   The Colonies Grow 4

Chapter Summary 5   Road to Independence 5

Chapter Summary 6   The American Revolution 6

Chapter Summary 7   A More Perfect Union 7

Chapter Summary 8   A New Nation 8

Chapter Summary 9   The Jefferson Era 9

Chapter Summary 10   Growth and Expansion 10

Chapter Summary 11   The Jackson Era 11

Chapter Summary 12   Manifest Destiny 12

Chapter Summary 13   North and South 13

Chapter Summary 14   The Age of Reform 14

Chapter Summary 15   Road to Civil War 15

Chapter Summary 16   The Civil War 16

Chapter Summary 17   Reconstruction and Its Aftermath 17

Chapter Summary 18   The Western Frontier 18

Chapter Summary 19   The Growth of Industry 19

Chapter Summary 20   Toward an Urban America 20

Chapter Summary 21   Progressive Reforms 21

Chapter Summary 22   Overseas Expansion 22

Chapter Summary 23   World War I 23

Chapter Summary 24   The Jazz Age 24

Chapter Summary 25   The Great Depression and FDR 25

Chapter Summary 26   World War II 26

Chapter Summary 27   The Cold War Era 27

Chapter Summary 28   America in the Fifties 28

Chapter Summary 29   The Civil Rights Era 29

Chapter Summary 30   Vietnam War Years 30

Chapter Summary 31   Search for Stability 31

Chapter Summary 32   New Challenges 32

Answer Key 33

★ **Chapter Summary 1**

The First Americans

People lived in the Americas for thousands of years before Christopher Columbus's voyage. Scientists believe the first Americans came from Asia by crossing a land bridge that once connected Alaska and Asia. The early Americans were nomadic hunters and gatherers. About 9,000 years ago, people discovered how to grow maize, or corn, and other crops. They no longer had to move from place to place, searching for food. Agriculture provided a reliable food supply and allowed people to form permanent communities.

The Maya, the Aztec, and the Inca civilizations flourished before A.D. 1500. Each empire covered hundreds of miles and included millions of people. The Maya built cities dominated by pyramids in Central American jungles and made advances in astronomy. The Aztec conquered almost all of Mexico by the 1400s. They built causeways to connect their lake capital with the shore. In the 1400s the Inca built at least 10,000 miles (16,000 km) of roads to connect the parts of their huge South American empire. They created walled terraces that allowed them to farm on mountain slopes. Varied cultures flourished in North America by adapting to the environment. The Hohokam dug irrigation channels to irrigate the desert. The Anasazi built cliff dwellings which were easily defended and offered shelter in bad weather. Mound Builders in central North America built thousands of earthen mounds for burial chambers and religious ceremonies. The Inuit in the Arctic lived in houses made of snow blocks. Pacific coast groups fished. Plains Native Americans were nomadic hunters. The people of the eastern woodlands formed complex political systems.

★ **THINK**
About It

DIRECTIONS: Use the information in the reading to answer the following question on a separate sheet of paper.

The Maya and Aztec created calenders. Why would a reliable calender be important to agriculture?

★ **Chapter Summary 2**

Exploring the Americas

In the 1300s the Renaissance, a period of great creativity, changed the way Europeans thought about the world and paved the way for an age of exploration. Powerful nations set out to find new trade routes to Asia and to acquire wealth. Scientific instruments like the astrolabe and the magnetic compass and new ship designs made long ocean voyages possible. As more explorations took place, mapmakers produced more accurate maps.

Between A.D. 300 and 1600, Ghana, Mali, and the Songhai Empire flourished in Africa south of the Sahara. Portugal grew rich from trade in gold, ivory, and slaves on West Africa's Gold Coast. Portugal's Vasco da Gama reached Asia by sailing east around Africa's southern tip. Christopher Columbus, sailing for Spain, thought he could find a sea route to Asia by sailing west across the Atlantic Ocean. In 1492 he landed in the Americas. In 1519 Ferdinand Magellan's crew began a journey in which they would circumnavigate the world.

Spanish conquistadors conquered Native American civilizations and built an American empire. Aided by horses and guns, the Spanish defeated the Aztec and Inca Empires, which also lost many people to European diseases for which Native Americans had no immunity. Spain used Native Americans and later African Americans as enslaved labor in mines and on plantations. Trade in goods and ideas between Europe and America, known as the Columbian Exchange, altered life on both sides of the Atlantic Ocean.

France, England, and the Netherlands also founded colonies in North America. Each country searched for a northwest passage to Asia—a water route through the Americas. Religious conflicts between Catholic and Protestant countries and trade rivalries spilled over to the colonies. French and Dutch explorers were more interested in setting up profitable trading posts than in establishing permanent settlements.

★ THINK
—*About It*

DIRECTIONS: Use the information in the reading to answer the following question on a separate sheet of paper.

Why do you think the French, English, and Dutch focused their efforts in North America?

Colonial America

After a difficult winter at Roanoke, Virginia, the first English colonists returned home. A second group later abandoned a Roanoke settlement and were never found. The first permanent English settlement at Jamestown prospered after John Rolfe persuaded the colonists to grow tobacco. In 1619 the colony's investors gave males the right to elect representatives, or burgesses, to a lawmaking assembly. This assembly, the House of Burgesses, became a model for colonial governments. In 1619 a Dutch ship brought the first Africans to the colonies. Although the first African laborers probably came as servants, later Africans became unwilling passengers on ships bound for America and were enslaved.

Pilgrims and Puritans came to America to escape religious persecution. They settled in Massachusetts but lacked tolerance of other religious beliefs. Settlers seeking religious freedom left to start Connecticut, Rhode Island, and New Hampshire. The Middle Colonies—New York, Pennsylvania, New Jersey, and Delaware—had the most diverse populations. Each attracted varied groups by offering religious freedom. People from the Netherlands, Sweden, and Germany settled in these colonies. New York at first belonged to the Dutch, who bought Manhattan and named it New Amsterdam. William Penn, America's first town planner, designed the city of Philadelphia. To protect Catholics in Maryland in the Southern Colonies, Lord Baltimore passed the Act of Toleration granting religious freedom. Small farmers from Virginia's backcountry settled North Carolina. Wealthy, slaveholding planters settled South Carolina. James Oglethorpe planned Georgia as a colony where debtors could start afresh.

France had more interest in establishing fur trading posts than in permanent settlements. Spain built forts in Texas as a buffer between New Spain and French claims. Junípero Serra founded the first Catholic missions in California.

★ THINK
About It

DIRECTIONS: Use the information in the reading to answer the following question on a separate sheet of paper.

Why did the English settlements develop into 13 separate colonies rather than one large colony?

★ Chapter Summary 4

The Colonies Grow

New England shipping linked the colonies with the world through a trading pattern called the *triangular trade.* These trade routes brought enslaved Africans to the colonies. On the first leg colonists shipped raw goods to the West Indies and traded for molasses, used to make rum. On the second leg they exchanged rum for enslaved people in West Africa. On the third leg traders sold enslaved West Africans for more molasses in the West Indies. The Middle Passage, the route leg which shipped enslaved Africans to the West Indies, was the most inhumane aspect of the route.

Because large plantations in the Tidewater region of the South needed many workers, planters there came to rely on slave labor. In the backcountry of the Appalachian Mountains, however, families farmed small plots of land and usually did not rely on slave labor. The injustice of slavery sparked debate in the colonies.

Other tensions developed in the colonies. The Navigation Acts of the 1650s prohibited colonists from sending goods on foreign ships or selling certain products to nations other than Great Britain. These laws angered colonists because they reduced profits from trade. In the colonies only white men who owned property had the right to vote. In North America, Great Britain and France competed for wealth and power, leading to conflict over resources and land. Different Native American groups formed alliances with Great Britain or France, and the Iroquois played one side against the other. In time the Iroquois gave certain trading rights to the British and upset the balance of power between France and Great Britain in the Americas, leading to the French and Indian War.

The Albany Plan of Union, a cooperative plan for defense of the colonies against the French, called for a unified elected government. Every colony rejected it. The French and Indian War ended with Great Britain in control of North America east of the Mississippi River. Chief Pontiac formed a Native American alliance which tried unsuccessfully to drive settlers from the western territories. To prevent conflict between Native Americans and colonists, King George III called a halt to further westward expansion by passing the Proclamation of 1763.

★ THINK
—About It

DIRECTIONS: Use the information in the reading to answer the following question on a separate sheet of paper.

Why might the individual colonies have rejected the Albany Plan of Union?

★ **Chapter Summary 5**

Road to Independence

The French and Indian War left Great Britain deeply in debt. The king looked to the colonies for revenue and instituted new taxes. When the colonists tried to avoid the taxes, writs of assistance allowed the British to search colonists' homes for smuggled goods on which no taxes had been paid. The Sugar Act set up courts to enforce anti-smuggling laws. The Stamp Act taxed almost all printed materials in the colonies. The colonists protested that Parliament had no right to tax them if they could not vote for its members. They boycotted British goods. Great Britain repealed the Stamp Act but imposed import taxes on basic items. The colonists responded with another boycott. Tensions mounted.

Parliament sent British troops to Boston. In 1770 British soldiers fired on a mob killing five colonists. The colonists called this the Boston Massacre and used propaganda to spread anti-British feelings. Seeking compromise, Great Britain repealed import taxes on all goods except tea. The Tea Act of 1773 gave a British company an unfair tax advantage over colonial merchants. At the "Boston Tea Party," colonists dumped British tea into the harbor. Parliament passed laws punishing the people of Boston. Colonists called these laws the Intolerable Acts. Many colonists became convinced that it was time to unite against the British.

In 1774 the First Continental Congress drafted a statement of grievances and voted to form militias. In 1775 British troops fought colonial militia at the battles of Lexington and Concord. The war for independence had begun. In June 1775, British and colonial forces clashed at the Battle of Bunker Hill. Although the British won, the Americans had fought hard. The Second Continental Congress created an army and sent a petition asking the king to protect their rights. When it was rejected, other battles took place. Delegates to the Congress signed the Declaration of Independence on July 4, 1776, proclaiming a new nation.

★ **THINK**
About It

DIRECTIONS: Use the information in the reading to answer the following question on a separate sheet of paper.

Why would Great Britain believe that colonists should help pay the costs of the French and Indian War?

★ Chapter Summary 6

The American Revolution

At first Great Britain seemed to have a huge advantage in the war. They had the world's finest navy and a trained army. The Patriots were inexperienced volunteers. One of every five Americans was a Loyalist. Some supported the king for religious reasons. Others depended on Great Britain for jobs or thought colonial grievances did not justify rebellion. Some feared the disorder of revolution. Great Britain hoped for a decisive victory that would bring a quick end to the war. Their plan to cut New England off from the Middle Colonies failed, however, when the Patriots forced a British army to surrender at Saratoga in 1777. This battle marked a turning point in the war and helped bring support from Great Britain's European rivals, most notably France.

The Patriots' darkest hour was the bitter winter of 1777–1778 at Valley Forge. Other pressures added to the colonists' problems. During the war women had to assume new responsibilities such as managing family farms or businesses. Angered by the colonists' desire to push westward, many Native Americans sided with Great Britain against the colonists. At sea the United States had to rely on privateers to attack the royal fleet since there was no American navy. The American victory at Saratoga forced the British to change strategy. They moved south and won several victories. The Americans responded by using hit-and-run tactics.

In 1781 a Patriot army, under the command of George Washington, moved quickly south. Aided by French troops and ships, the Americans surprised General Charles Cornwallis's army at Yorktown and forced it to surrender. Great Britain granted the colonies independence in the Treaty of Paris in 1783, and the war for American independence ended.

Even though Great Britain had superior military strength, the Americans won the war. The revolution was a people's movement, and Americans were fighting on their own land. The Patriots received help from France and Spain and had a great leader in George Washington.

★ THINK
About It

DIRECTIONS: Use the information in the reading to answer the following question on a separate sheet of paper.

Why would a victory, like Saratoga, make other nations more willing to support the Americans?

★ **Chapter Summary 7**

A More Perfect Union

Many challenges remained for the new nation after the end of the Revolutionary War. Americans set up a republic, a government in which citizens rule through elected officials. The Articles of Confederation created a weak national government that could not regulate trade, impose taxes to pay debts, or make states obey its laws. Instability followed.

In 1787 state delegates met to address the problems. This Constitutional Convention drafted a Constitution calling for a strong central government, including a chief executive to enforce national laws, a court system, and a two-house legislature. One house, called the Senate, included two members from each state. The other house, called the House of Representatives, included members from each state based on the state's population.

The Framers of the Constitution believed that the government is based on a contract between people and a ruler, and worried about a central government that might become too powerful. To limit government power, they separated the central government into branches and built in checks and balances. Congress, the legislative branch, makes laws. The executive branch, headed by the president, carries out the laws. Courts make up the judicial branch which makes sure that laws passed by lawmakers and signed by the president are constitutional. The Framers left many important powers to the states. Sharing of powers between a national government and states is called federalism.

Federalists who supported the Constitution feared that without a strong government there would be chaos. Opponents feared a strong government could take away individual liberties. For the Constitution to become law, 9 of the 13 states had to ratify, or approve, it. All 13 states voted to ratify. Antifederalists won guarantees that a bill of rights, protecting individual freedoms, would be added to the Constitution as amendments, or changes.

★ **THINK**
About It

DIRECTIONS: Use the information in the reading to answer the following question on a separate sheet of paper.

Why would Americans fear giving too much power to one person or a strong central government?

★ **Chapter Summary 8**

A New Nation

In 1789 George Washington became the first president. That same year Congress created executive departments. The heads of these departments made up the president's cabinet. Congress also set up the Supreme Court and other federal courts with the power to reverse state court rulings.

In 1791 the Bill of Rights was added to the Constitution. These 10 amendments guaranteed personal liberties. Secretary of the Treasury Alexander Hamilton found ways to pay government debts and strengthen the nation's economy. Congress approved a plan for the nation's new capital to be located in the South.

In 1794 Washington used a show of force to end the Whiskey Rebellion, in which farmers protested a federal tax. He also used the army and treaties to end Native American resistance to settlements in Ohio. When France and Great Britain went to war, Washington maintained American neutrality. He set precedents by not seeking a third presidential term and by publishing his Farewell Address in which he warned against the formation of political parties and permanent alliances with foreign nations.

Politicians formed parties nonetheless. Federalists stood for strong central government. Democratic-Republicans wanted power left in the hands of the states. Federalist John Adams was elected president in 1796. In the XYZ affair, French agents demanded a bribe to stop seizing American ships. This led to an undeclared naval war with France that lasted two years. Federalists in Congress passed controversial laws. One, the Alien Act, allowed the president to deport aliens he thought were dangerous. Another, the Sedition Act, made false or malicious criticism of the government illegal. Republicans drafted a theory of states' rights, called the Virginia and Kentucky Resolutions, saying that states could legally overturn federal laws they thought were unconstitutional.

★ **THINK**
——*About It*

DIRECTIONS: Use the information in the reading to answer the following question on a separate sheet of paper.

What parts of the Bill of Rights might possibly conflict with the Sedition Act?

★ **Chapter Summary 9**

The Jefferson Era

In 1800 Republicans Thomas Jefferson and Aaron Burr each received 73 electoral votes for president. The House of Representatives had to decide the election. It elected Jefferson president. To prevent future electoral ties, the Twelfth Amendment was passed. In *Marbury* v. *Madison,* Chief Justice John Marshall ruled that a law made by Congress was unconstitutional. This established judicial review—the right of the Supreme Court to check the acts of other government branches.

In 1803 Jefferson bought the Louisiana Territory from France. These vast lands ran from the Mississippi River to the Rocky Mountains. The purchase doubled the size of the nation. Meriwether Lewis and William Clark explored the Louisiana Territory and gained valuable information on the people, plants, animals, and geography of the West.

Great Britain seized American sailors to serve in its navy. This impressment angered people. To avoid war, Congress passed the Embargo Act, banning trade with other countries. It hurt the economy and Jefferson's popularity. James Madison, a Republican, became president in 1809.

Meanwhile, conflict with Native Americans grew in the West. Shawnee Chief Tecumseh organized a confederacy of Native American nations. In 1811 William Henry Harrison won fame by attacking a Native American village at the Battle of Tippecanoe. Hopes for a Native American confederacy died when Tecumseh was killed.

Pressured by young Republican War Hawks, Congress declared war on Great Britain in 1812. Although attempts to conquer Canada failed, American ships won the Battle of Lake Erie. In 1814 the British burned the capital, Washington, D.C. The British then sailed to Baltimore where Francis Scott Key wrote "The Star-Spangled Banner." Unaware the war was over, troops fought the Battle of New Orleans in 1815. It made Andrew Jackson a hero.

★ **THINK**
About It

DIRECTIONS: Use the information in the reading to answer the following question on a separate sheet of paper.

How might the presence of Sacagawea, a Native American woman, have helped Lewis and Clark?

★ **Chapter Summary 10**

Growth and Expansion

In the late 1700s inventors created machines that performed work previously done by hand. In Great Britain people began leaving their homes to work in mills. This period is called the Industrial Revolution. Around 1800, the Industrial Revolution took root in the United States. New Englanders built factories which brought all the manufacturing stages together in one place. Use of interchangeable parts made mass production possible. In the South the cotton gin revolutionized agriculture. Factories made Americans less dependent on imported goods and strengthened the nation's economy. Industrialization spurred the growth of cities. Along with this development came many urban problems such as overcrowding, unsanitary conditions, disease, and the threat of fire.

Improvements in technology revolutionized transportation. Steamboats made shipping goods and passengers cheaper and faster. Canals—artificial waterways—were built uniting the East and the West. Towns sprang up along the canal routes. Settlers moved west in waves, leading to the admission of nine new states.

James Monroe became president in 1817. A period followed known as the Era of Good Feelings because Americans maintained a sense of unity. Sectionalism or loyalty to one's region, intensified after 1820. Regional representatives argued over slavery, tariffs, and internal improvements such as canals and roads. John Calhoun of the South championed states' rights. Daniel Webster of the North spoke against sectionalism. Henry Clay of the West tried to settle sectional disputes. In 1820 he proposed the Missouri Compromise to resolve sectional tension over the admission of new states to the Union. The Missouri Compromise admitted Missouri as a slave state and Maine as a free state. It also banned slavery in territories north of the 36°30′ parallel.

Monroe's administration settled land disputes with Great Britain and Spain. Simón Bolívar and José de San Martín liberated South America from Spain. The Monroe Doctrine declared that the United States would oppose any new European colonies in the Americas.

★ **THINK**
About It

DIRECTIONS: Use the information in the reading to answer the following question on a separate sheet of paper.

Why would Henry Clay of the West be in favor of internal improvements?

★ **Chapter Summary 11**

The Jackson Era

In 1824 no presidential candidate won a majority of the electoral votes. When the House of Representatives chose John Quincy Adams, Andrew Jackson's supporters claimed that Adams had made a corrupt deal to win the presidency. In 1828 Democratic-Republicans from the South and the West, who favored states' rights, supported Jackson. National Republicans, from the Northeast, wanted a strong central government. They supported Adams. Jackson won the bitter presidential election. By 1828 people from Western states and workers doubled the number of voters. Most new voters admired Jackson as a self-made man.

Jackson replaced many federal workers with his supporters, the practice became known as the "spoils system." He gave citizens more say in politics by supporting *nominating conventions* where delegates picked candidates. He stopped South Carolina from seceding, or leaving the Union, over a high tariff by threatening military action. The Indian Removal Act allowed the government to force Native Americans from southeastern lands. Jackson ignored a Supreme Court ruling in favor of the Cherokee. The Cherokee and three other groups of Native Americans sadly moved to the Indian Territory west of the Mississippi River in a long march called the Trail of Tears. The Seminole fought until the government gave up efforts to move them.

The Bank of the United States controlled the nation's money supply. Jackson thought it helped the rich and hurt the poor. He forced the bank to close. Martin Van Buren, his vice president, succeeded Jackson in 1837. An economic depression began with the Panic of 1837. It turned people against the Democrats. William Henry Harrison, a Whig, was elected president in 1840.

★ **THINK**
About It

DIRECTIONS: Use the information in the reading to answer the following question on a separate sheet of paper.

Why would Northern manufacturers favor a high tariff, or tax paid on imported goods?

★ **Chapter Summary 12**

Manifest Destiny

The Oregon country covered a vast area in the Pacific Northwest. Fur traders, called mountain men, were the first Americans to settle there. In the 1840s thousands of pioneers traveled the Oregon Trail seeking land and opportunity. Manifest Destiny—the idea that the United States had a special mission to extend its borders to the Pacific—also contributed to this migration west.

James K. Polk, a believer in Manifest Destiny, became president in 1845. Americans in Texas won independence from Mexico in 1836. In the spirit of Manifest Destiny, Texas was admitted as a slave state in 1845.

After 1821 American traders traveled the Santa Fe Trail to New Mexico. Trade brought settlers to the area. Others, lured by glowing accounts of the harbors, climate, and land, pushed on to California. When Mexico refused to sell these provinces, Polk provoked a war. After a skirmish in disputed land, he claimed Mexican soldiers had attacked troops on American soil. Congress declared war in 1846. The Mexican War divided American public opinion, but it was a victory for Manifest Destiny. In the 1848 Mexican Cession, the United States acquired New Mexico and California. The 1853 Gadsden Purchase of Southwest lands extended the nation to its modern borders between the Atlantic Ocean and the Pacific Ocean south of Canada and north of Mexico.

In 1848 gold was found in California. Thousands of prospectors rushed to California. Few struck it rich, but many stayed to farm or open businesses. In 1850 California became a free state. Mormons migrated to Utah to avoid religious persecution. Mormons resisted federal authority until Utah became a state in 1896.

★ **THINK**
——About It

DIRECTIONS: Use the information in the reading to answer the following question on a separate sheet of paper.

Why might people fleeing religious persecution choose a harsh, barren area in which to settle?

★ **Chapter Summary 13**

North and South

Industrialization dramatically changed the North. Mass production of textiles began in New England in the early 1800s. Waterpower or steam power allowed factories to make goods at lower costs. Steamboats transformed travel on inland waterways. Clipper ships set speed records on the oceans. Steam-powered trains linked the Midwest and the East. New towns and industries sprang up along the routes. The telegraph allowed people to communicate instantly. The steel plow, the reaper, and the thresher turned the Great Plains into an agricultural empire. As factory conditions worsened, workers formed unions and staged strikes for higher pay and improved safety. African Americans and women were denied equal rights due to discrimination.

Immigration to the United States increased dramatically between 1840 and 1860. A potato famine brought 1.5 million Irish immigrants to the United States. Most worked in cities. More than one million Germans immigrated; many settled in the Midwest. Immigrants enriched the culture, but nativists felt they threatened native-born Americans. Nativists formed the American Party, which became known as the Know-Nothing Party.

The textile industry created a huge demand for cotton. The cotton gin made large harvests possible. A few Southerners tried to encourage industry, but profits from agriculture kept the South rural and dependent on cotton. Southern plantations were largely self-contained units and included the planter's home, workshops, and cabins for enslaved workers. Most enslaved people worked in fields under the supervision of an overseer and lived in appalling conditions. Slave codes—harsh rules—made their lives more difficult. A few escaped on the Underground Railroad, a network of safe houses owned by opponents of slavery. By the mid-1800s the South had many cities. These cities provided free African Americans with opportunities to form their own communities. Although spared the horrors of slavery, free African Americans were denied an equal share in economic and political life.

★ **THINK**
About It

DIRECTIONS: Use the information in the reading to answer the following question on a separate sheet of paper.

How might the cotton gin have increased the demand for slave labor?

★ **Chapter Summary 14**

The Age of Reform

In the early 1800s a reforming spirit arose in the United States. Religious leaders called on people to become more spiritual and to work to improve society. Temperance workers crusaded against alcohol abuse. Educational reformers convinced states to adopt the principles of free public education, improve schools, and train teachers. Dorothea Dix worked to improve care for the mentally ill. Higher education slowly became available to women, African Americans, and people with disabilities.

The changes in American society influenced art and literature. Artists chose distinctly American subjects. Writers explored American themes and styles. The number of abolitionists, reformers who wanted to end slavery, grew rapidly. In the 1830s abolitionists lectured and wrote about the evils of slavery. They began calling for the immediate emancipation, or freeing, of enslaved people. Some worked on the Underground Railroad, a network of safe houses where escaping slaves could stay as they fled north. Abolitionism split the nation. Many Southerners believed the movement threatened their way of life. Some Northerners feared that abolitionists would cause civil war.

Gender prejudice among abolitionists drove female reformers to become the first feminists, people who work for women's rights. A women's rights convention was held at Seneca Falls, New York, in 1848. It issued a statement calling for an end to laws that discriminated against women and demanding suffrage, the right to vote. Beginning with Wyoming in 1890, states began granting woman suffrage. Reformers broke down many barriers to equal education and employment for women. They also won reform of property laws and divorce laws.

★ **THINK**
About It

DIRECTIONS: Use the information in the reading to answer the following question on a separate sheet of paper.

Why would travelers on the Underground Railroad call the houses where they stayed "stations"?

★ **Chapter Summary 15**

Road to Civil War

The rift between the North and the South widened in the mid-1800s. It appeared that Oregon, New Mexico, and Utah would become free states, upsetting the balance between free and slave states. Southerners talked of secession—leaving the Union. The Compromise of 1850 removed restrictions on slavery in the New Mexico territory. It required states to return fugitives— runaway enslaved persons—to their holders. Many Northerners refused to obey the Fugitive Slave Act. A novel, *Uncle Tom's Cabin*, added to antislavery feeling. The Kansas-Nebraska Act of 1854 tried for a compromise. It let people in the territories settle the slavery issue by popular sovereignty, or voting on the issue. Disputed elections in Kansas led to violence. People on both sides died. A new party, the Republicans, vowed to end slavery in the territories. In the *Dred Scott* case, the Supreme Court ruled that enslaved persons were property and that slavery could not be prohibited, angering many Northerners.

Republican Abraham Lincoln won fame debating Stephen Douglas about slavery. In 1860 Democratic presidential nominee Douglas said he would refuse to protect slavery in the territories. John Breckinridge ran as a proslavery candidate. Republicans nominated Lincoln and vowed to oppose slavery in the territories. Voting went along sectional lines; Lincoln won. In December 1860 South Carolina seceded. Six more states also seceded to form the Confederacy. They elected Jefferson Davis president. Lincoln vowed not to allow secession. In April 1861 Confederates shelled Fort Sumter, South Carolina. Lincoln called for volunteers to defend the Union. Four more states seceded. The Civil War had begun.

★ **THINK**
—*About It*

DIRECTIONS: Use the information in the reading to answer the following question on a separate sheet of paper.

Why would admitting three free states and no new slave states to the Union concern Southerners?

★ **Chapter Summary 16**

The Civil War

Four slave states bordering the North and the South did not secede. Because of their strategic locations, Abraham Lincoln avoided antagonizing these border states. Both sides had advantages and disadvantages. The North had more people and industry, better railroads, and Lincoln's leadership. Southern soldiers were fighting on their own land to protect their way of life. At first the South had better generals. To restore the Union, the North planned to blockade Southern ports, gain control of the Mississippi River, and seize Richmond, the Confederate capital. To win independence, the South planned to defend its land until the North tired of war.

Despite early Southern victories, the war in the East turned into a bloody stalemate. In the West the Union slowly won control of the Mississippi River despite heavy casualties. The Northern blockade cut Southern trade and kept ammunition in short supply for the South.

On January 1, 1863, Lincoln issued the Emancipation Proclamation. It stated that any persons held as slaves within any state in rebellion were free. He hoped this would weaken European support for the South. African Americans made up 10 percent of the Union forces. Both sides suffered horrendous losses—dead and wounded. Inflation and income taxes caused hardships in both regions. In July 1863, the Union won major victories at Gettysburg in the East and Vicksburg in the West. Its armies marched through the South in 1864 destroying everything that could be of use to the enemy. Southern general Robert E. Lee surrendered to General Ulysses S. Grant in April 1865. Soon after, the war ended.

More than 600,000 soldiers died in the Civil War. In the South damages ran to billions of dollars. The war, however, ended the idea of secession and freed millions of African Americans.

★ **THINK**
About It

DIRECTIONS: Use the information in the reading to answer the following question on a separate sheet of paper.

In 1863 why would Lincoln limit the Emancipation Proclamation to states that had seceded?

★ Chapter Summary 17

Reconstruction and Its Aftermath

Reconstruction refers both to the period in which the South was rebuilt and to the various plans for rebuilding. Abraham Lincoln wanted to give generous terms to the South to encourage an orderly restoration of the Union. Radical Republicans in Congress, though, wanted to punish the South.

Lincoln was assassinated in 1865. President Andrew Johnson's plan required less change in the South than Lincoln's plan. The new Southern state governments passed black codes, depriving African Americans of their civil rights. Congress, over Johnson's veto, nullified the codes and passed constitutional amendments guaranteeing equal rights. Radical Republicans took charge of Reconstruction. They placed Southern states under military authority and required that they ratify the Fourteenth—"equal rights"— Amendment. They impeached Johnson, but fell one vote short of removing him from office.

In 1869 war hero Ulysses S. Grant became president. During Reconstruction African Americans held major political offices. Southern education improved and industry grew. A few Reconstruction officials were corrupt, but most were not. Still, the Ku Klux Klan burned homes and murdered African Americans and whites in the South. In the North citizens tired of Reconstruction. Corruption in Grant's administration split Republicans, and Democrats regained control in the South. New Southern leaders, the "Redeemers," encouraged industry, but cut social services. Poll taxes and literacy tests kept poor African Americans from voting, but "grandfather clauses" exempted whites. Jim Crow laws established segregation. In *Plessy* v. *Ferguson* (1896), the Supreme Court ruled that "separate but equal" facilities were legal.

★ THINK
About It

DIRECTIONS: Use the information in the reading to answer the following question on a separate sheet of paper.

Why would white Southerners be more likely to vote for Democrats after the Civil War?

★ Chapter Summary 18

The Western Frontier

In the 1850s prospectors went west in search of gold. Boomtowns sprang up around mining sites. Few struck it rich, but many stayed to work in new industries such as mining companies that extracted metals for manufacturers. Frontier lands around the boomtowns eventually became states, and government money and land grants helped railroads expand. By 1869 a transcontinental rail line spanned the continent. As railroads brought workers west and carried goods east, towns grew along the tracks. Demand for beef in the East and railroad expansion created a Cattle Kingdom in the Southwest. Ranchers drove herds to towns where cattle could be shipped east by rail. A price collapse, overgrazing, and cold winters in the 1880s helped end the Cattle Kingdom.

In 1862 Congress passed the Homestead Act. Settlers earned ownership of land by agreeing to farm it. Thousands of homesteaders came. Many were widows or single women who had the same property rights as men. The government tried to force nomadic Plains Native Americans to become farmers by moving them to reservations. Abuses in the management of reservations led to conflicts. A series of battles took place. The massacre of more than 300 Lakota Sioux at Wounded Knee in 1890 marked the end of the Native Americans' struggle to maintain their way of life.

In the late 1800s farmers suffered from falling prices and rising costs. They blamed manufacturers, railroads, and banks. In 1892 farmers helped form the Populist Party. Populists wanted a system based on free silver—unlimited production of silver coins to help farmers pay debts. Their crusade failed, but some of their goals—an eight hour workday, an income tax, the secret ballot, and direct election of senators—became law.

★ THINK
—*About It*

DIRECTIONS: Use the information in the reading to answer the following question on a separate sheet of paper.

How might the arrival of thousands of small farmers lead to the end of the Cattle Kingdom?

★ **Chapter Summary 19**

The Growth of Industry

After 1865 railroads changed the nation. They carried settlers west and rural dwellers to cities. They took raw materials to factories and finished goods to markets. They hired thousands. By consolidating—combining separate companies—a few powerful men controlled rail lines. These railroad barons used rebates—secret discounts—to bankrupt smaller companies. They made secret agreements which led to higher rates. These practices brought calls for government regulation, but the laws had little effect.

Between 1860 and 1890, the government granted more than 400,000 patents for inventions. They included the telephone, the vacuum cleaner, and the light bulb. Factories, streetlights, and living room lamps ran on electricity. After 1900 the automobile and the airplane ushered in modern transportation.

Companies raised money by forming corporations and selling stock to investors. The oil and steel industries grew rapidly. Mergers—combining of companies—concentrated power in a few giant corporations. These trusts gained monopolies—total control—over an industry. They spurred economic growth, but people argued that, without competition, there was no reason to control prices or improve goods and services. The Sherman Antitrust Act banned trusts and monopolies but was ineffective.

Industrial growth in the late 1800s created jobs and raised the standard of living, but workers paid a price for economic progress. Working in factories and mines was unhealthy and unsafe. Workers organized unions to demand better pay and working conditions. The Knights of Labor recruited women, African Americans, immigrants, and unskilled laborers. Violence and failures marred the early labor movement, but it did win some gains, and it did not die out.

★ **THINK**
About It

DIRECTIONS: Use the information in the reading to answer the following question on a separate sheet of paper.

How would the automobile and the airplane spur the growth of the oil and steel industries?

★ **Chapter Summary 20**

Toward an Urban America

After 1865 millions of new immigrants came to the United States. Most came from eastern and southern Europe. Thousands more came from China and Japan. Many were pushed by poverty or persecution, and others were pulled by hopes of opportunity. Those with contagious diseases were denied entry. Few of the new immigrants spoke English. Most worked as unskilled laborers and gathered in urban neighborhoods with people of their own nationality. Many immigrants encountered hostility. Ethnic, religious, and racial tensions caused problems, and led to violence, but an expanding economy needed these workers. The immigrants enriched American culture with their religions, language, literature, and customs.

Industrialization also brought rural Americans to cities. By 1910 almost half of Americans were urban dwellers. Cities offered jobs, stores, and entertainment. While the poorest people—including most immigrants—lived in tenements—apartments in slums—the middle class lived comfortably, many of them in suburbs. The wealthy lived in mansions and threw extravagant parties. Growing cities became overcrowded, unhealthy, and crime ridden. These problems fostered a spirit of reform.

Many tried to help the poor. Some wrote books showing the horrendous conditions in tenements. Others opened settlement houses that offered medical care, nurseries, and language classes. Advocates of progressive education taught citizenship and hands-on activities as well as memorization of knowledge.

Creativity flourished in other areas. Architects built skyscrapers with steel supports and elevators. Writers and artists used realism to explore new themes and subjects. African Americans developed a new kind of music—jazz. Watching sports, vaudeville shows, and the movies became popular pastimes.

★ THINK
—*About It*

DIRECTIONS: Use the information in the reading to answer the following question on a separate sheet of paper.

Why were skyscrapers necessary to the growth of big cities?

★ **Chapter Summary 21**

Progressive Reforms

In the late 1800s and early 1900s, progressive reformers fought against political corruption, urban problems, and business abuses. Investigative reporters called *muckrakers* helped progressives by publishing shocking "exposes" that caught the public's eye. Progressive reforms included the creation of the civil service system, the government of cities by commissions, and the introduction of direct primary elections. Progressives also worked for more power for voters, direct election of senators, and regulation of business.

During the Progressive Era, the roles of women changed in American society. More women earned college degrees and started careers outside the home. Many emerged as reform leaders. They started clubs which helped workers, children, immigrants, and the poor. They also won passage of the Nineteenth Amendment to the Constitution which granted woman suffrage—the right to vote—in 1920. In 1919 the Eighteenth Amendment banned the manufacture or sale of alcoholic beverages. President Theodore Roosevelt was a progressive. He earned the nickname "trustbuster" by regulating railroad, beef, tobacco, and oil monopolies. He also took steps to conserve natural resources.

His successor, William Howard Taft, disappointed progressives in the fields of tariffs and conservation. The Republican Party split in 1912. Progressives formed their own party in 1912 and nominated Roosevelt for president. The three-way race helped Democrat Woodrow Wilson become president. Wilson won some progressive victories, but the movement was losing momentum. Progressive reforms did little to end racial or religious discrimination. African Americans, Hispanic Americans, and Native Americans formed their own groups. These groups took steps to gain equal opportunity and improve the lives of minorities.

★ **THINK**
—*About It*

DIRECTIONS: Use the information in the reading to answer the following question on a separate sheet of paper.

Why do you think the Eighteenth Amendment is often referred to as the *Prohibition Law*?

★ **Chapter Summary 22**

Overseas Expansion

In the late 1800s European empires exerted political and economic control over weaker regions. Some Americans thought the United States should also practice imperialism. These Americans wanted new markets and new lands. Others wanted to spread Christianity and Western civilization. In 1853 the United States pressured Japan into a trade agreement. In 1867 it purchased Alaska from Russia. Trade with Latin America grew.

A modern navy and Pacific bases were needed to protect these American interests. The nation acquired the Midway islands and Samoa. After American sugar growers ousted Queen Liliuokalani of Hawaii, the United States annexed Hawaii in 1898. Other countries agreed to an Open Door policy in China after a nationalist uprising—the Boxer Rebellion. Japan emerged from the Russo-Japanese War as the strongest naval power in the Pacific. The United States's "Great White Fleet" sailed around the world to demonstrate American sea power.

When Spain brutally put down several Cuban revolts in the late 1800s, yellow journalists fueled American anger at the act, which ultimately led to the Spanish-American War (1898). The war began after the American ship, the *Maine*, mysteriously exploded in Havana Harbor. With Spain's surrender, the United States acquired Puerto Rico, Guam, and the Philippines. Cuba, though independent, came under American control. The United States then supported Panamanian independence and rented land there to build the Panama Canal. Opened in 1914, the canal connects the Atlantic Ocean with the Pacific Ocean.

The Roosevelt Corollary asserted that the United States had a right to act as a "policeman" and protect order in Latin America. To protect American business, the United States sent troops to the Dominican Republic, Cuba, and Mexico. The troop deployment caused resentment in Latin America.

★ **THINK**
—About It

DIRECTIONS: Use the information in the reading to answer the following question on a separate sheet of paper.

Why would bases in the middle of the Pacific Ocean be important during this period?

★ Chapter Summary 23

World War I

Nationalism—feelings of intense loyalty to one's country—and imperialism, militarism, and rival alliances led to international instability in Europe. Ethnic groups demanded their own nations. In 1914 Gavrilo Princip, a Serbian nationalist, assassinated the Austro-Hungarian heir, Archduke Franz Ferdinand and his wife. That act drew nations in rival alliances into war. The Allies were led by Great Britain, France, and Russia; the Central Powers were led by Germany, Austria-Hungary, and the Ottoman Empire. Japan, and later Italy, joined the Allies.

Western Europe endured three years of trench warfare. New weapons, like machine guns and poison gas, caused huge losses. The United States tried to stay neutral. Allied propaganda—information designed to influence opinion—and trade won American support. Then a German submarine sank the British liner, *Lusitania*. Among the dead were 128 Americans. In 1917 the United States intercepted a secret German telegram—the Zimmermann telegram—which promised support to Mexico if it attacked the United States. Spurred by these events, the United States joined the Allies on April 6, 1917. The military drafted 3 million Americans; 2 million others volunteered.

Communists overthrew the democratic government in 1917 and took Russia out of the war. American troops helped drive the Germans from France. Germany surrendered, and an armistice—an agreement to stop fighting—was signed on November 11, 1918.

During the course of the war, Americans had bought war bonds and endured rationing, which limited goods available to consumers. Opponents of the war were portrayed as unpatriotic. Criticizing the government was banned. German Americans were persecuted. President Woodrow Wilson outlined a just peace in his Fourteen Points, but the Allies wanted revenge. The Treaty of Versailles imposed harsh terms on Germany. The Senate rejected the treaty and refused to join a peacekeeping League of Nations.

★ THINK
—About It

DIRECTIONS: Use the information in the reading to answer the following question on a separate sheet of paper.

Why did President Wilson need Senate approval of the treaty and the League of Nations?

★ Chapter Summary 24

The Jazz Age

In 1919 anarchists—people who believe there should be no government—sent bombs to public officials. People worried that communism threatened American institutions. People suspected of being "Reds," or Communists, were arrested and deported. The Red Scare passed, but fear of foreigners and radicals remained.

The fear also affected the labor movement. Strikers were accused of being "Red agitators," antiunion sentiment grew, and union membership fell. Racial tension led to violence, including a Chicago riot. In 1920 Republican presidential candidate Warren G. Harding promised a return to "normalcy," but scandals plagued President Harding's administration. The most notorious involved the leasing of government oil reserves at Teapot Dome. When Harding died in 1923, his vice president, Calvin Coolidge, succeeded him. Both Warren Harding and Calvin Coolidge believed in laissez-faire economics and low business taxes. They opposed involvement in international affairs but sought peace.

Many Americans prospered in the 1920s, and American lifestyles changed. Employers set up safety and health insurance programs. Installment buying allowed people to buy automobiles. The "car culture" emerged." Car trips and commuting became part of life. Almost 4 million Americans worked in auto-related jobs. Farmers, however, did not share in the prosperity.

Women won the right to vote and pursued new careers. "Flappers" became a symbol of liberated women. Radio, movies, and jazz contributed to changing attitudes which clashed with traditional values. The Eighteenth Amendment established Prohibition—a ban on the manufacture and sale of alcohol—and inadvertently set the stage for the growth of organized crime. Criminal organizations engaged in *bootlegging*—making and selling illegal alcohol—which customers drank in *speakeasies.* The Twenty-first Amendment repealed Prohibition.

Teaching evolution, the theory that humans evolved over vast periods, led to religious controversy. Nativism reemerged and led to laws limiting the number of immigrants.

★ THINK
—About It

DIRECTIONS: Use the information in the reading to answer the following question on a separate sheet of paper.

What kinds of businesses would increased driving on roads and highways create?

★ Chapter Summary 25

The Depression and FDR

Stock values fell in 1929. Investors, who had bought stocks on credit, tried to sell, but prices started to fall below what they had paid. On October 24, "Black Thursday," the stock market crashed. Large banks, businesses, and individuals lost huge amounts of money. Like dominoes the cornerstones of the economy began to topple. Unemployment rose as sales fell. Small banks suffered when farmers could not repay loans. As banks failed and closed, depositors lost their savings. By 1932, 25 percent of Americans were unemployed. Millions more had to work for lower wages, and many lost their homes. The Great Depression had begun. President Herbert Hoover took too little action too late.

Democrat Franklin D. Roosevelt (FDR) defeated Hoover in the 1932 presidential election. FDR told the nation that "the only thing we have to fear is fear itself." He promised a New Deal. Lawmakers passed laws to regulate and aid banks. New Deal programs provided jobs and relief. These programs brought electricity to rural areas and helped farmers. Some New Deal programs built hospitals, schools, and other public works. One insured savings accounts. Another created the Social Security system. The New Deal did not end the Depression, but it restored public faith in the economy. Families still struggled to survive. Although socialism and communism promised to end economic and racial injustice, they did not become major political forces. Still more than half the African Americans in the South had no jobs. Many Mexican Americans were expelled from the country.

Despite criticism of the New Deal, FDR was reelected in 1936. Conservative and wealthy people attacked him as a radical trying to destroy free enterprise. Others, who proposed radical ways to redistribute the wealth, complained that the New Deal did not do enough. More New Deal programs further expanded the federal government's economic and social role. Unions grew stronger during the Depression.

★ THINK
About It

DIRECTIONS: Use the information in the reading to answer the following question on a separate sheet of paper.

What Depression-era pressures would cause the government to expel Mexican Americans from the country?

★ Chapter Summary 26

World War II

After World War I, ruthless men used public anger and suffering to gain power in Europe and Asia. Fascist dictators, who had extremely nationalistic and racist views, arose in Italy and Germany. Italy invaded Ethiopia. German dictator Adolf Hitler annexed neighboring lands. The Nazis, led by Hitler, blamed Germany's domestic problems on Jews. In Japan military leaders invaded China.

Hoping to avoid being drawn into the conflicts, the United States passed a series of Neutrality Acts. Other nations also tried to avoid war, but in 1939 Hitler seized Czechoslovakia and attacked Poland. Great Britain and France declared war. By 1940 Denmark, Norway, the Netherlands, Belgium, and France had fallen to the Nazis. Fascist governments in Italy, Germany, and Japan formed the Axis Powers.

While vowing neutrality, Franklin D. Roosevelt prepared for war. Arms and supplies were sent to Great Britain. A draft law was passed. Oil sales to Japan stopped. On December 7, 1941, Japan bombed the American base at Pearl Harbor, Hawaii. The attack destroyed the Pacific fleet and killed more than 2,000 Americans. A unified nation mobilized with amazing speed. More than 15 million Americans served in the armed forces. Industry and civilians sacrificed together. Production soared, ending the Great Depression. Although there was no evidence that they were disloyal, more than 100,000 Japanese Americans were sent to detention centers.

Eventually the Nazis were driven from Africa and Russia. Italy fell. By early 1945, Western Europe was liberated. But the war had left a grim inheritance. Allied troops discovered the results of the Holocaust—the Nazi campaign that systematically murdered 6 million Jews and millions of others. A defeated Hitler committed suicide. German leaders signed a surrender, and May 8, 1945, was declared "Victory in Europe," or V-E Day.

The war in the Pacific region continued. The United States won control of the Pacific by island-hopping—capturing key islands and advancing on Japan. When the United States dropped two atomic bombs on two different Japanese cities in August 1945, the terrible loss of life and destruction prompted Japan to surrender. One week later, the most destructive war in history was over.

★ THINK
About It

> **DIRECTIONS:** Use the information in the reading to answer the following question on a separate sheet of paper.
>
> What tradition did Franklin D. Roosevelt break by running for president in 1940?

★ **Chapter Summary 27**

The Cold War Era

In 1945 Soviet forces occupied much of Eastern Europe. The United States tried to "contain," or stop, the spread of communism. It gave massive financial aid to help Western European countries rebuild their economies and resist communism. The Berlin airlift broke a Soviet blockade by flying food and fuel to that city after Soviet leader Joseph Stalin blockaded the city. The United States and the Soviet Union were in a cold war. Instead of fighting, each tried to intimidate the other by building military power and forming alliances. They also competed for influence in Asia and Africa. Civil war in China ended with a Communist government in control.

Congress passed the GI Bill of Rights in 1944. This law gave veterans loans for college, job training, and buying homes. Inflation led to labor strikes. President Harry Truman tried to continue FDR's reform policies, but a Republican Congress blocked him. It moved to control unions, cut spending, and reduce regulation of business. Truman desegregated the armed forces and ended discrimination in federal jobs.

In 1950 Communist North Korea invaded non-Communist South Korea. American troops fought with a United Nations (UN) force which liberated the South. When UN forces invaded North Korea, China attacked them. The war became a stalemate. It ended in 1953 with neither side winning.

The cold war intensified fear of communism, especially after the Soviets developed an atomic bomb in 1949. Employers and Congress investigated people. Some lost jobs. Senator Joseph McCarthy made unfounded charges against innocent people. In 1954 the Senate censured—formally criticized—McCarthy for improper conduct.

★ **THINK**
— *About It*

DIRECTIONS: Use the information in the reading to answer the following question on a separate sheet of paper.

Why do you think the United States and the Soviet Union were called the superpowers after 1949?

★ **Chapter Summary 28**

America in the Fifties

By 1952 Americans worried about communism and blamed the Democrats for the Korean stalemate. They elected Republican Dwight D. Eisenhower, a World War II hero, as president. Voters trusted "Ike." He pledged to end the Korean War and follow moderate "middle-of-the-road" policies at home. His administration created 40,000 miles (64,000 km) of interstate highways that spurred economic growth. Eisenhower continued many New Deal programs. He expanded Social Security and increased the minimum wage. In 1959 Alaska and Hawaii became states.

A policy of "massive retaliation," reliance on nuclear weapons, led to an arms race. Soviet-backed Egypt seized the Suez Canal, but diplomatic moves avoided a conflict between the superpowers. The Soviets launched *Sputnik*, the first satellite, in 1957. Fidel Castro overthrew a dictator in Cuba and became a Soviet ally. Eisenhower and Soviet leader, Nikita Khrushchev, discussed peaceful coexistence—the idea that the superpowers could have differences but avoid war. Retiring in 1961, Eisenhower warned that an alliance between military and industrial leaders to build expensive weapons could endanger American liberties.

Government spending and technology created an economic boom that raised the standard of living in the 1950s. A "baby boom" increased the population by nearly 20 percent. Mass production of homes led to suburban growth. Television and rock 'n' roll dominated entertainment. The generation gap referred to differing attitudes of parents and children. Farmers, migrant workers, and minorities did not share in the prosperity. Some Americans criticized materialism—a focus on money and possessions rather than on spiritual values. Others described the frustrations of women and African Americans.

★ **THINK**
   About It

DIRECTIONS: Use the information in the reading to answer the following question on a separate sheet of paper.

What effect might Eisenhower's highway program have had on the economic power of railroads?

★ **Chapter Summary 29**

The Civil Rights Era

In 1960 President John F. Kennedy promised to help the poor and the elderly. Peace Corps volunteers worked in poor countries. Congress failed to pass Kennedy's bills for education, job training, and civil rights. His assassination in 1963 stunned the nation and led to theories of a conspiracy.

New president Lyndon B. Johnson convinced Congress to pass his ambitious reform plan—the Great Society. Head Start provided preschool education for the poor. The Job Corps offered job training. Medicare and Medicaid helped pay for medical care.

African Americans won major victories. In 1954 the Supreme Court banned segregation in schools in *Brown* v. *Board of Education of Topeka, Kansas*. Rulings that desegregated transportation and public places followed. Martin Luther King, Jr., emerged as a civil rights leader during a bus boycott in Montgomery, Alabama. King organized nonviolent protests. Sit-ins began in the 1960s. Civil rights protesters would sit in stores and not leave until they were served. Violence against demonstrators won them national support. In 1963, more than 200,000 Americans marched for civil rights in Washington, D.C. Congress passed the Civil Rights Act of 1964 and the Voting Rights Act of 1965. Both banned discrimination. Radical voices emerged. Some called for separate societies; others urged revolution. In the mid-1960s riots erupted in more than 40 cities. The 1968 assassination of Martin Luther King, Jr., set off rioting in more than 100 cities.

Women also made gains. The 1963 Equal Pay Act outlawed paying women less than men for performing the same jobs. They won seats in Congress and on the Supreme Court. Hispanic Americans, Native Americans, and the disabled won more economic and political power as laws were passed to protect their rights.

★ THINK
About It

DIRECTIONS: Use the information in the reading to answer the following question on a separate sheet of paper.

How would John F. Kennedy's assassination have helped Lyndon Johnson convince Congress to pass civil rights laws?

★ **Chapter Summary 30**

The Vietnam Era

President John F. Kennedy increased spending on nuclear arms but also worked for a nuclear test ban. He countered the Communist appeal to the poor by sending aid to Latin America, Africa, and Asia. In 1961 the Soviets built a wall separating East and West Berlin. That year an American-backed invasion of Cuba—the Bay of Pigs—was a disaster. In 1962 Soviet nuclear bases in Cuba led to confrontation. A compromise ended the Cuban missile crisis. Kennedy and Soviet leader Nikita Khrushchev took steps to reduce the chances of nuclear war and signed a nuclear test ban treaty.

Communist North Vietnam and non-Communist South Vietnam had been at war since 1959. President Dwight D. Eisenhower and President John F. Kennedy both sent aid and military advisers to support the unpopular government of the South. To prevent its fall, President Lyndon B. Johnson claimed the Communists had attacked American ships and increased involvement. By 1967, more than 500,000 American troops were in Vietnam, but the jungle hindered troop movements. The Vietcong, Communist guerrillas, blended in with civilians.

Massive bombing failed to end the war. Antiwar activists (doves) organized college protests and burned their draft cards. War supporters (hawks) viewed them as anti-American. Both sides criticized Johnson. In 1968 the Communists launched the Tet offensive. Although it was a turning point, it turned many more Americans against the war. Americans lost faith in their government. Martin Luther King, Jr., and dove leader Robert Kennedy were assassinated, and Johnson retired. After Republican Richard Nixon was elected, he called for expanded bombing, a more active South Vietnamese role in the war, and gradual withdrawal of Americans. Six students died in antiwar protests. After peace talks ended American involvement in 1973, South Vietnam fell to the Communists.

★ **THINK**
—*About It*

DIRECTIONS: Use the information in the reading to answer the following question on a separate sheet of paper.

Why would Nixon's campaign theme— a return to "law and order" —appeal to voters in 1968?

★ **Chapter Summary 31**

Search for Stability

Richard Nixon developed détente—easing cold war tensions by finding areas of common interest. He improved relations with the People's Republic of China, believing this would force the Soviet Union to be more cooperative. Agreements with the Soviets limited some nuclear weapons and increased trade. A war in the Middle East tested détente, but the superpowers avoided direct involvement. Angered by American support for Israel, Arab nations banned oil shipments to the United States. Diplomacy helped end this embargo and ease tensions.

Nixon reduced the role of the federal government through New Federalism, which gave states more authority and resources. To curb inflation, he froze wages and prices, and he increased federal spending to spur growth. Neither measure cured the nation's economic woes.

Nixon resigned after the American public learned that he had ordered a cover-up of a break-in at Democratic offices. This Watergate scandal damaged Americans' faith in politics and the presidency. Gerald Ford promised an honest administration, but his popularity fell when he pardoned Nixon and offered amnesty to those who had illegally avoided the draft during the Vietnam War.

Détente continued under Ford, but so did inflation and unemployment at home. Jimmy Carter defeated Ford in 1976 by promising to end corruption, but policy reversals on economic problems made him appear indecisive. Carter based his foreign policy on human rights—a concern that governments around the world grant freedom without persecution—and mediated a peace agreement between Israel and Egypt. His inability to win the release of American hostages in Iran and renewed tensions with the Soviet Union, however, led to his defeat in 1980.

★ **THINK**
— *About It*

DIRECTIONS: Use the information in the reading to answer the following question on a separate sheet of paper.

Why would improved relations with China force the Soviet Union to be more cooperative?

★ **Chapter Summary 32**

New Challenges

Conservative views that government was too big, taxed too much, and spent too much won Ronald Reagan the presidency in 1980. He made government smaller by deregulation—cutting the rules government placed on businesses. He believed lower taxes would lead to greater investment in business and create jobs. Lower taxes, however, meant less revenue. To afford the tax cuts, Congress cut spending on social programs. At the same time, Reagan rejected détente and began a costly military buildup.

When Mikhail Gorbachev tried to reform communism, Soviet-American relations improved. George Bush became president in 1989. As cold war tensions eased, the nuclear powers agreed to destroy existing nuclear weapons for the first time.

Eastern European nations rebelled against communism and elected reform leaders. When the Soviet republics declared their independence, Gorbachev announced the end of the Soviet Union.

Bush's popularity had soared. Iraqi invaders were driven from Kuwait and the Persian Gulf War ended. When the failure of many savings and loan banks cost taxpayers $500 billion, however, and Bush refused to increase spending during a recession, his popularity fell.

In 1992 New Democrat Bill Clinton won the presidential election by stressing domestic economic issues. A gun control law passed, but a health-care reform plan did not. The United States, Canada, and Mexico agreed to end trade barriers, and Middle East peace accords were signed.

Republicans won control of Congress in 1994. When the two parties could not agree on budget cuts, the government shut down for 27 days. The dispute helped Clinton politically. He was reelected in 1996, although Republicans maintained control of Congress.

In Clinton's second term, a booming economy boosted his popularity. However, a scandal put his presidency in crisis. In December 1998, the House impeached Clinton for perjury and obstruction of justice. The Senate voted to acquit the president on both charges.

★ **THINK**
About It

> **DIRECTIONS:** Use the information in the reading to answer the following question on a separate sheet of paper.
>
> What do you think was the greatest challenge the nation faced between 1981 and the present?

Answer Key

★ CHAPTER 1

Answers may vary. One possible response: A calendar is important to farmers because they must know when to plant, how long to let a crop grow, and when to harvest the crop.

★ CHAPTER 2

Answers may vary. One possible response: The English, French, and Dutch focused on North America because the Spanish already controlled Central and South America. By concentrating on North America, they could avoid territorial disputes with the Spanish.

★ CHAPTER 3

Answers may vary. Possible responses include: The people who settled in the various colonies had different reasons for coming to America. Some wanted religious freedom. Others were seeking economic opportunity. Religious differences sometimes caused conflicts and even led to the founding of new colonies. Economic differences could also lead to conflicts that would divide colonies. Different ethnic backgrounds also might make it more difficult for the colonists to form one united colony.

★ CHAPTER 4

Answers may vary. One possible response: The Albany Plan of Union called for one elected government. If they agreed to the plan, each colony would have to give up some of its independence and cede some of its legislative powers to a central government.

★ CHAPTER 5

Answers may vary. One possible response: The French and Indian War had been fought in North America. Britain was fighting to protect its wealth and power,

but at the same time it was the lives, homes, and property of the colonists that British troops were protecting from French and Native American attacks.

★ CHAPTER 6

Answers may vary. One possible response: Other nations realized for the first time that the Patriots might win their independence from Britain. This possibility made it in their interest to support the nation that would control much of North America. As rivals of Britain, it was also in their interest to contribute to an effort that had a realistic chance of lessening Britain's wealth and power.

★ CHAPTER 7

Answers may vary. One possible response: Americans had just fought a war for independence in part because they believed that a powerful individual (the king) and a powerful central government (Parliament) had been taking away their liberties. They would be afraid that the same thing could happen if they gave too much power to a chief executive or to a national congress.

★ CHAPTER 8

Answers may vary. One possible response: The Sedition Act could possibly conflict with the parts of the Bill of Rights that guarantee freedom of speech and freedom of the press because it restricted what people could say or publish in a newspaper.

★ CHAPTER 9

Answers may vary. One possible response: Sacagawea may have been able to act as an interpreter for Lewis and Clark when they met Native American groups. She might also have been familiar with the geography and been able to guide them through unfamiliar or hazardous territory.

★ CHAPTER 10

Answers may vary. One possible response: Internal improvements like canals and roads brought settlers to the Western states. The influence of the West grew as it gained more seats in the House of Representatives. Internal improvements also strengthened the West's economy. These improvements made it easier for farmers to ship crops to eastern markets and for industry to spring up in towns along canals and roads.

★ CHAPTER 11

Answers may vary. One possible response: A high tariff or import tax added to the cost of imported goods and would make European products more expensive. This, in turn, would make goods produced by American manufacturers less expensive compared to imported goods.

★ CHAPTER 12

Answers may vary. One possible response: Because the land is harsh and barren, it is less likely to attract other settlers. Consequently, the people would be left alone to practice their religion without persecution.

★ CHAPTER 13

Answers may vary. One possible response: The cotton gin made large harvests possible and made growing cotton immensely profitable. This would lead to an increase in the number and size of plantations, thereby increasing the need for workers to plant and harvest the crop.

★ CHAPTER 14

Answers may vary. One possible response: Enslaved persons and abolitionists helping them escape needed to use code words to help them escape detection and capture. The term *Underground Railroad* is a code word. On railroads, stations are buildings along the route at which people can board trains or wait for the next scheduled departure to continue their journey. Thus the term "station" is an appropriate code word for a house at which escaping slaves can stay for a time before continuing north to freedom.

★ CHAPTER 15

Answers may vary. One possible response: The admission of three free states and no slave states would mean that proslavery forces would be badly outnumbered in the Senate. States are awarded seats in the House of Representatives based on population. Therefore new Western states with relatively small populations might have little effect on the balance of power in the House. However, every state has two seats in the Senate. Six new votes would give antislavery forces a decided advantage in the Senate.

★ CHAPTER 16

Answers may vary. One possible response: The outcome of the Civil War was still in doubt in 1863. Lincoln did not want to antagonize people in the slaveholding border states which had not seceded. Emancipating enslaved people everywhere might have gained support for prosecession sentiments in those states and hurt the North's chances of winning the war. If the North lost, Lincoln would not have the authority to free enslaved people in any slaveholding state.

★ CHAPTER 17

Answers may vary. One possible response: Antislavery forces had formed the Republican Party in the 1850s. A Republican, Abraham Lincoln, was president in 1860. His refusal to permit secession had led to the Civil War. Republicans controlled the federal government during the Civil War and Reconstruction. White Southerners, most of whom were former Confederates, would likely blame the Republicans for the South's defeat and its postwar problems. For these reasons, they would be more likely to vote for Democrats rather than Republicans.

★ CHAPTER 18

Answers may vary. One possible response: The cattle ranchers needed large land areas on which to graze their cattle and open range to drive them to market. The arrival of small farmers would deprive them of needed grazing space and increase opposition to cattle drives across private property on which crops had been planted.

★ CHAPTER 19

Answers may vary. One possible response: Automobile and airplane bodies and engines are usually made of steel. Oil is used to lubricate their motors. Oil is one of the components in gasoline which fuels automobile and airplane engines.

★ CHAPTER 20

Answers may vary. One possible response: Unlike frontier areas, cities had very limited room for outward expansion. Because space was limited, developers had to build upward rather than outward to expand. Skyscraper apartment houses could provide housing for large numbers in a small area, and skyscraper offices and stores could provide room for expanding businesses in a limited space.

★ CHAPTER 21

Answers may vary. One possible response: The Eighteenth Amendment is often referred to as the "Prohibition Law" because it prohibited the manufacture and sale of alcoholic beverages.

★ CHAPTER 22

Answers may vary. One possible response: Ships of the time traveling between the United States and Asia needed to refuel when crossing the ocean. The islands provided stations for refueling and repairs. They also provided bases from which military ships could respond more quickly to crises in Asia that involved American interests.

★ CHAPTER 23

Answers may vary. One possible response: The constitutional system of checks and balances gives the president the power to negotiate treaties, but it also gives the Senate the power to accept or reject the treaties the president makes.

★ CHAPTER 24

Answers may vary. One possible response: Increased driving would create a need for highway construction and road repair. It would also create a need for gas stations and auto-repair shops. Restaurants and motels would open to serve motorists along busy highways. Stores relocating to the suburbs would eventually lead to shopping malls.

★ CHAPTER 25

Answers may vary. One possible response: Millions of people could not find work during the Great Depression. The strain could very easily lead to a reemergence of the nativist feeling that Mexican immigrants were taking jobs from native-born Americans. This would place pressure on the government to limit and even reverse immigration.

★ CHAPTER 26

By 1940 Franklin D. Roosevelt, who was first elected in 1932, had already served two terms. By running in 1940, he broke the precedent set by George Washington of not seeking a third term as president. Eventually a law limiting presidents to two terms was passed by Congress.

★ CHAPTER 27

Answers may vary. One possible response: The United States had developed the atomic bomb by 1945. By 1949 the Soviet Union also had the atomic bomb. This weapon gave the two countries a weapon of mass destruction that other powers could not match. Thus they became known as "superpowers."

★ CHAPTER 28

Answers may vary. One possible response: The creation of the modern interstate highway system contributed to the decline of the railroads. Using the highways, people could now commute and vacation using their own automobiles rather than relying on trains. Long distance trucking firms could compete with the railroads in carrying goods to and from markets.

★ CHAPTER 29

Answers may vary. One possible response: John F. Kennedy had proposed a civil rights bill in 1963. Lyndon Johnson might have asked Congress to honor his memory by passing this bill which evokes American ideals of justice and equality.

★ CHAPTER 30

Answers may vary. One possible response: Many people longed for an end to the social disorder of antiwar demonstrations and assassinations. They might have viewed Richard M. Nixon's campaign theme as a pledge to end the turmoil and return the nation to the order and conformity of the 1950s.

★ CHAPTER 31

Answers will vary. Students should recognize that improved Chinese-American relations would strengthen American and weaken Soviet influence in Asia. They should also understand that a Chinese-American alliance would threaten the Soviet Union in the event of a military conflict. Therefore, it was in Soviet interests to increase ties with the United States and preserve a balance of power among these three large nations as opposed to being excluded from the easing of tensions.

★ CHAPTER 32

Answers will vary but might include government regulation, a costly military buildup, the breakup of the Soviet Union and resulting shifts in world power, the Persian Gulf War, or the presidential impeachment.